Kitab Sirr al-Asrar Wa Mazhar al-Anwar

THE BOOK OF THE SECRET OF SECRETS AND THE MANIFESTATION OF LIGHTS

Shaikh Abdul Qadir Jilani
(May Allah be pleased with him)

Tr. By: Shaikh Muhammad ibn Yahya at-Tadifi al-Hanbalion

KITAB BHAVAN
New Delhi - 110 002 (INDIA)

Name of the book : Sirr al-Asrar Wa Mazhar al-Anwar - The Book of the secrets of secrets And the Manifestation of Lights

Written by : Shaikh Abdul Qadir Jilani

Translated by : Shaikh Muhammad ibn Yahya at-Tadifi al-Hanbalion

2nd Edition : 2017

ISBN : 81-7151-388-3

Book Code : K00072

Printed & Published by: Nusrat Ali Nasri for Kitab Bhavan
Moonis Ali Nasri for Kitab Bhavan
1784, Kalan Mahal, Darya Ganj, New Delhi-110002

PRINTED IN INDIA

If you have any corrections, comments, or questions about this publication, please feel free to contact us.

CONTENTS

PREFACE AND LINES OF DESCENT

In the Name of Allah, the All-Merciful, the All-Compassionate.
Bismi'llahi'r-Rahmani'r-Rahim.

Praise be to Allah, the All-Powerful, the All-Knowing, the All-Wise, the All-Generous, the Noble, the Compassionate Lord, the One who revealed the Wise Remembrance and the Glorious Qur'an to the Envoy, whom He sent to convey the Right Religion and the Straight Path.

Blessing and peace be on the seal of the Mission, the guide out of error, and on the Messenger ennobled with the noblest of the Scriptures and the Book, Muhammad, the unlettered Prophet, the Arabian, the trustworthy, and on his family, the rightly guided guides, and his Companions, the excellent elite, and may Allah grant them peace in great abundance.

This book contains the words of the Supreme Helper, the Lordly Cardinal Pole, the everlasting edifice, the radiantly shining lamp, the Sultan of the saints and the masters of direct knowledge, the proof of the chosen and those who have reached their spiritual destination, Allah's Gray Falcon, our patron, our master and our exemplary guide to Allah (Exalted is He), the noble highborn patrician, the chieftain, Shaikh Muhyi'd-Din 'Abd al-Qadir al-Jilani al-Hasani al-Husaini (may Allah sanctify his splendid innermost being, and may He illuminate his noble mausoleum), son of Imam Sayyid Abu Salih Musa Jangi Dost, son of Imam Sayyid 'Abdu'llah, son of Imam Sayyid Yahya az-Zahid, son of Imam Sayyid Muhammad, son of Imam Sayyid Dawud, son of Imam Sayyid Musa, son of Imam Sayyid 'Abdu'llah, son of Imam Sayyid Musa al-Jawn, son of Imam Sayyid 'Abdu'llah al-Mahd, son of Imam Sayyid al-Hasan al-Muthanna, son of Imam al-Hammam Sayyid al-Hasan as-Sibt, son of our chief and our patron, the Commander of the Believers, Abu'l-Husain 'Ali ibn Abi Talib (may Allah be well pleased with them all).

On his mother's side of the family, the line of descent of our revered master and patron, Shaikh Muhyi'd-Din 'Abd al-Qadir al-Jilani (may Allah the Exalted be well pleased with him), is as follows:

He is Suyyid Shaikh Muhyi'd-Din 'Abd al-Qadir al-Jilani (may Allah sanctify his luminous innermost being), son of Sayyida Umm al-Khair Amat al-Jabbar Fatima, daughter of Sayyid 'Abdu'llah as-Sawma'i az-Zahid, son of Sayyid Abu 'Abdi'llah Jamal ad-Din Muhammad, son of Sayyid Mahmud, son of Sayyid Abu'l-'Ata' 'Abdu'llah, son of Sayyid Kamal ad-Din 'Isa, son of Sayyid Imam Abu 'Abdi'llah 'Ala' ad-Din Muhammad al-Jawad, son of Sayyid Imam 'Ali ar-Rida, son of Sayyid Imam Musa al-Kazim, son of Imam Ja'far as-Sadiq, son of Imam Muhammad al-Baqir, son of Imam Zain al-'Abidin 'Ali, son of Imam al-Hammam al-Husain, the Martyr of Karbala', son of Imam al-Hammam, the Commander of the Believers, our master 'Ali ibn Abi Talib (may Allah be well pleased with him, and with them all).

* * *

Knowledge is the most noble talent, the most magnificent degree, the most splendid object of pride, and the most valuable form of merchandise, since it is the means by which to arrive at the realization and affirmation of the Oneness of the Lord of All the Worlds [tawhid Rabb al-'alamin], and belief in His Prophets and Messengers (may Allah's blessings be upon them all).

The religious scholars became the favoured elite of the servants of Allah. He drew them toward the signs of His religion and guided them toward it. He preferred them and selected them for the special merit of grace. They are the heirs and deputies of the Prophets, and the chieftains and confidants of the Messengers As Allah (Exalted is He) has said:

Then We gave the Book as inheritance to those thumma awrathna'l-Kitaba'lladhi whom We elected of Our servants.

nastafaina min 'ibadi-na: But of them are some who wrong themselves fa-min-hum zalimun li-nafsi-h: and of them are some who adopt a middle course, wa min-hum muqtasid.

(That is to say: "There are some whose bad deeds are on a par with their good deeds.")

and of them are some wa min-hum sabiqun who outstrip through good deeds. bi'l-khairi. (35:32)

As the Prophet (Allah bless him and give him peace) once said:

"The religious scholars are the heirs of the Prophets in knowledge. The inhabitants of heaven will love them, and the fish in the sea will seek forgiveness on their behalf, until the Day of Resurrection."

Allah (Exalted is He) has also said:

Only those of His servants fear Allah who have knowledge. innama yakhsha'llaha min 'ibadi-hi'l-'ulama'. (35:28)

The Prophet (blessing and peace be upon him) also said:

"Allah will raise up His creatures on the Day of Resurrection, then He will distinguish the scholars, for Allah (Exalted is He) will say: 'O company of scholars, when I instilled My knowledge in you, I did so only because of My knowledge of you. I did not instil it in you so that I might torment you. Away you go, to the Garden of Paradise, for I have forgiven you!'"

Praise be to Allah, the Lord of All the Worlds, in every situation. Praise be to the One who has established the ascending levels as a protection for the worshipful servants, and the stations of nearness for those who know by experience.

One of the seekers requested us to compile a manuscript for him, sufficient for all essential purposes. We have therefore compiled this summary for his benefit, in accordance with his wish, so that it may be enough to satisfy him and others. I have given it the title: "The Secret of Secrets, concerning what is needed by the righteous [Sirr al-Asrar fi-ma yahtaju ilai-hi'l-abrar]."

INTRODUCTION

THE BEGINNING OF CREATION [IBTIDA' AL-KHALQ]

You should know—may Allah enable you to achieve what is dear and pleasing to Him!-that Allah (Exalted is He) first created the spirit of Muhammad (Allah bless him and give him peace) from the light of His Beauty. As Allah (Almighty and Glorious is He) has told us:

I created the spirit of Muhammad (Allah bless him and give him peace) from the light of My countenance.

As the Prophet (Allah bless him and give him peace) has said:

The first thing that Allah created was my spirit [ruh]. The first thing that Allah created was my light [nur]. The first thing that Allah created was the pen [qalam]. The first thing that Allah created was the intellect ['aql].

This means that they are all one thing, that being the Muhammadan Reality [al-Haqiqat al-Muhammadiyya], but it is called a "light [nur]" because it is pure and unclouded by the darknesses of Majesty. As Allah (Blessed and Exalted is He) has said:

There has now come to you from Allah qad ja'a-kum mina'llahi a Light, and a clear Book. Nurun wa Kitabun mubin. (5:15)

It is also called an "intellect ['aql]," because it comprehends universal truths [kulliyyat]. It is also called a "pen [qalam]," because it is an instrument for the transmission of knowledge, just as the pen is an instrument in the realm of letters [of the alphabet].

The Muhammadan spirit is thus the quintessence of all entities, the first of all beings and the origin of them all. As he has said (blessing and peace be upon him):

I am from Allah and the believers are from me.

Allah created all the spirits from him in the realm of Divinity [Lahut], and in the finest real formation. "Muhammad" is the name of all human beings in that realm, and he is the original home.

Then, when four thousand years had passed, Allah created the Heavenly Throne ['Arsh] from the light of the eye of Muhammad (Allah bless him and give him peace), and from the Heavenly Throne He created the rest of existing entities. Then He reduced the spirits to the lowest level of existence, meaning the physical bodies. As Allah (Exalted is He) has said:

Then We reduced him [the human being] thumma radadna-hu to the lowest of the low. asfala safilin. (95:5)

In other words, the first descent was from the realm of Divinity [Lahut] to the realm of Omnipotence [Jabarut]. Between the two Sanctuaries, Allah (Exalted is He) clothed them with the light of Omnipotence, which is the royal spirit [ruh sultani]. Then he sent them down, in this attire, to the realm of Sovereignty [Malakut], and He clothed them with the light of Sovereignty, which is the immaterial spirit [ruh ruhani]. Then He sent them down to the realm of Dominion [Mulk], and He clothed them with the light of Dominion, which is the physical spirit. Then from it Allah created the bodies. As He has said (Exalted is He):

Out of it [the earth] We created you, min-ha khalaqna-kum and into it We shall send you back again, wa fi-ha nu'idu-kum and We shall bring you forth from it a second time. wa min-ha nukhriju-kum taratan ukhra. (20:55)

Then Allah (Exalted is He) commanded the spirits to enter the bodies, so they entered at Allah's command (Exalted is He). As He has said (Almighty and Glorious is He):

And I breathed into him of My Spirit. wa nafakhtu fi-hi min Ruhi. (38:72)

When the spirits became attached to the physical bodies, they forgot the covenant they had contracted on the day when Allah asked them: "Am I not your Lord?" and they said: "Yes indeed!" Because of this, they did not return to the original home, but the All-Merciful Source of Help took pity on them. He sent down Heavenly Books to remind them of that original home. As He has said (Exalted is He):

We sent Moses with Our signs, [saying]: wa la-qad arsalna Musa bi-ayati-na "Bring your people forth from darkness into light, an akhrij qawma-ka mina'z-zulumati ila'n-nuri and remind them of the days of Allah." wa dhakkir-hum bi-ayyami'llah. (14:5)

In other words: "Remind them of the former days of communion with Him, in the company of the spirits."

All the Prophets came into this world and went away to the Hereafter because of this admonition, but few human beings took heed, longed for their original home and returned to it, until Prophethood was assigned to the supreme Muhammadan spirit, the seal of the Mission and the guide away from error. Allah sent him to those heedless people, to open their eyes from the sleep of heedlessness, so he summoned them to Allah (Exalted is He), to contact with Him and the meeting with His sempiternal Beauty. As Allah (Exalted is He) said to him:

Say: "This is my way: I call to Allah qul hadhihi sabili ad'u ila'llah: with insightful knowledge, I and whoever follows me." 'ala basiratin ana wa mani'ttaba'a-ni. (12:108)

The Prophet (Allah bless him and give him peace) once said:

My Companions are like the stars. Whomever of them you follow, you will be guided aright.

Insight comes from the eye of the spirit, which opens within the heart of the saints [awliya']. That is why it is not acquired by knowledge of the external world, but only by knowledge of the inner Presence. As Allah (Exalted is He) has said:

And We taught him knowledge from Our Presence. wa 'allamna-hu min ladun-na'ilma. (18:65)

It is therefore necessary for the human being to acquire that eye, and so become one of the masters of insight, by taking instruction from a saint, a spiritual guide whose teaching concerns the realm of Divinity [Lahut].

O brethren! Wake up, and hasten to forgiveness from your Lord through repentance! As Allah (Exalted is He) has said:

And hasten to forgiveness from your Lord, wa sari'u ila maghfiratin min Rabbi-kum and a Garden as wide as the heavens and the earth, wa jannatin 'ardu-ha's-samawatu wa'l-ardu which has been made ready for those who are truly devout. u'iddat li'l-muttaqin. (3:133)

Embark upon the path, and return to your Lord with these spiritual caravans. The path will soon be cut off, and no travelling companion will be found. We have not come to settle in this vile, dilapidated world, nor for the sake of eating, drinking, and satisfying crude natural instincts. Your Prophet is waiting, sorrowful for your sake.

As he said (peace be upon him):

My sorrow is for the members of my Community who will come in later times.

The knowledge that is sent down to us is two-fold: exoteric and esoteric, meaning the sacred law [shari'a] and direct understanding [ma'rifa]. Allah (Exalted is He) has commanded us to apply the sacred law to our outer being, and direct understanding to our inner being, so that the combination of the two will result in knowledge of Reality [Haqiqa], just as fruit is produced by the tree and the leaves. As Allah (Exalted is He) has said:

He has partitioned the two seas. maraja'l-bahraini. They meet, [but] between them there is a barrier yaltaqiyan: baina-huma barzakhun that they do not overpass. la yabghiyan. (55:19,20)

Reality cannot be attained, and the goal cannot be reached, by exoteric knowledge alone. Perfect worship is accomplished by means of both forms of knowledge, not one without the other. As Allah (Exalted is He) has said:

I did not create the jinn and humankind wa ma khalaqtu'l-jinna wa'l-insa except to worship Me. illa li-ya'budun. (51:56)

In other words: "to know and understand Me." If someone does not know and understand Him, how can he worship Him? Direct knowledge is attainable only by removing of the veil of the lower self [nafs] from the mirror of the heart, and cleaning and polishing that mirror. It will then reflect the beauty of the treasure hidden in the secret of the heart's core. Allah (Exalted is He) has said in the Sacred Tradition [Hadith Qudsi]:

I was a hidden treasure and I wished to be known, so I created Creation.

It is clear, therefore, that Allah (Exalted is He) created the human being to know and understand Him.

Direct knowledge is of two kinds: knowledge of the attributes [sifat] of Allah (Exalted is He), and knowledge of His Essence [Dhat]. Knowledge of the attributes is experienced by the physical body in both domains [this world and the Hereafter], while knowledge of the Essence is experienced by the holy spirit in the Hereafter. As Allah (Exalted is He) has said:

And We supported him [Jesus] with the holy spirit. wa ayyadna-hu bi-Ruhi'l-Qudus. (2:87)

They [who know the Essence] are likewise supported with the holy spirit.

These two experiences are attainable only by means of two forms of knowledge, the exoteric knowledge and the esoteric knowledge mentioned above. As the Prophet (peace be upon him) once said:

Knowledge ['ilm] is two-fold: knowledge conveyed by the tongue, that being Allah's testimony to His servants, and knowledge conveyed by the heart, that being the knowledge that is useful for the attainment of the goal.

First of all, the human being needs knowledge of the sacred law, in order to provide the body with sufficient education in the realm of the attributes, that being the realm of the stages of development. He then needs esoteric knowledge, in order to provide the spirit with education in its own realm of understanding. That can only be achieved by abstaining from all practices that are incompatible with the sacred law and the spiritual path [tariqa]. Its achievement requires the endurance of personal and spiritual hardships, for the sake of pleasing Allah (Exalted is He), without hypocritical display [riya'] and the pursuit of fame [sum'a]. As Allah (Exalted is He) has said:

So whoever hopes for the meeting with his Lord, fa-man kana yarju liqa'a Rabbi-hi let him do righteous work, fa-l'-ya'mal 'amalan salihan and let him give no one any share at all wa la yushrik in the worship due unto his Lord. bi-'ibadati Rabbi-hi ahada. (18:110)

The realm of direct knowledge is the realm of Divinity [Lahut], and that is the original home, in which the holy spirit was created in the finest formation. What is meant by the holy spirit is the real human spirit, which was installed in the core of the heart, and which becomes manifest through repentance, instruction, and constantly declaring: "There is no god but Allah [la ilaha illa'llah]." This declaration is first made with the tongue, then with the inner being, when the heart has become alive.

The Sufis have called the inner being "the child of the spiritual concepts [tifl al-ma'ani]," because it arises from the sacred conceptions. It is called a child for several reasons:

1. It is born from the heart, as the child is born from the mother, then reared by the father as it steadily grows to maturity.

2. Just as worldly knowledge is taught to ordinary children, spiritual knowledge is taught to this special child.

3. The ordinary child is unsoiled by the filth of external sins, and this special child is likewise pure and unstained by the filth of polytheism [shirk], heedlessness and physicality.

4. In the case of this special child, the purity of form is even greater, so it is seen in dreams in a shape like that of the angels.

5. Allah (Exalted is He) has described the attendants of the Garden of Paradise in terms of childhood [tifliyya], in His saying (Almighty and Glorious is He):

There wait on them immortal boys. yatufu 'ala-him wildanun mukhalladun. (56:17)

And there go round, waiting on them, wa yatufu 'alai-him young boys of theirs, ghilmanun la-hum as if they were hidden pearls. ka-anna-hum lu'lu'un maknun. (52:24)

6. The name "child" conveys a sense of its gentleness and its cleanliness.

7. The name "child" is used metaphorically, to indicate its connection with the body and its likeness to the human form, but only for the sake of comparison, not for the purpose of belittlement. It refers to this "child's" initial state. This "child" is the real human being, because he has a connection

with Allah (Exalted is He), so the body and physicality are not unlawful to him. As the Prophet (Allah bless him and give him peace) once said:

I have a time with Allah, when there is no space for any angel brought near [to the Lord], nor for any Prophet sent as a Messenger.

This [Prophet sent as a Messenger] refers to the human nature of the Prophet (Allah bless him and give him peace). The angel brought near [to the Lord] refers to his spirituality, which was created from the light of Omnipotence [Jabarut], as was the angel, so it has no entry into the light of Divinity [Lahut]. The Prophet (blessing and peace be upon him) also said:

Allah has a Garden in which there are no houries, no palaces, no honey and no milk, but where one gazes only at Allah's countenance (Exalted is He).

As Allah (Magnificent is His Majesty) has said:

Faces on that day will be resplendent, wujuhun yawma'idhin nadira: looking toward their Lord. ila Rabbi-ha nazira. (75:22,23)

As the Prophet (peace be upon him) said:

You will see your Lord as you see the moon on the night when it is full.

If the angel and the physical body entered into these realms, they would be burned to ashes. As Allah (Exalted is He) has said in the Sacred Tradition [Hadith Qudsi]:

If I disclosed the splendours of My Majesty, I would burn up everything as far as My eye can see.

As Gabriel (peace be upon him) said: "If I had drawn nearer by a fingertip, I would have been set on fire."

FIRST SECTION

The Return Of The Human Being To His Original Home, By Three Stages.

There are two aspects to the human being: the physical [jusmani] and the spiritual [ruhani]. The physical aspect is common to ordinary human beings, while the spiritual aspect is peculiar to special human beings.

For the ordinary human being, the return to his home proceeds by stages, based on the practical implementation of knowledge of the sacred law [shari'a], the spiritual path [tariqa] and direct experience [ma'rifa]. As the Prophet (peace be upon him) has said:

Comprehensive wisdom is direct experience of the Truth, so long as it is practiced without hypocritical display and the pursuit of fame.

The stages are on three levels:

1. The Garden in the realm of Dominion [Mulk], that being the Garden of Shelter [Ma'wa].

2. The Garden in the realm of Sovereignty [Malakut], that being the Garden of Bliss [Na'im].

3. The Garden in the realm of Omnipotence [Jabarut], that being the Garden of Paradise [Firdaws].

These are the bounties of the physical aspect, so the body can only reach its goal by means of three corresponding forms of knowledge: the sacred law, the spiritual path and direct experience. As the Prophet (peace be upon him) has said:

Comprehensive wisdom is direct experience of the Truth and putting it into practice, and recognizing falsehood and forsaking it.

He also said (peace be upon him):

O Allah, let us see the Truth as true, and enable us to follow it. Let us see falsehood as false, and enable us to avoid it.

-and:

If someone knows himself, he knows his Lord and his Creator and complies with His command.

In the case of the special human being, his destination is nearness [to Allah], and his return is by means of knowledge of Reality [Haqiqa], that being the affirmation of Oneness [Tawhid] in the realm of Divinity [Lahut]. By means of his regular practice, he can experience this nearness during his life in this world, whether he be asleep or awake. When the body is asleep, the heart finds an opportunity to escape to its original home, either wholly or in part. As Allah (Exalted is He) has said:

Allah receives souls at the time of their death, Allahu yatawaffa'l-anfusa hina mawti-ha and that which has not yet died in its sleep. wa'llati lam tamut fi manami-ha: He keeps that for which He has ordained death, fa-yumsiku'llati qada 'alai-ha'l-mawta and dismisses the rest till an appointed term. wa yursilu'l-ukhra ila ajalin musamma. (39:42)

That is why the Prophet (blessing and peace be upon him) once said:

The sleep of the scholar is better than the worship of the ignoramus.

This state is experienced after the heart has been enlivened by the light of the affirmation of Oneness, and after constant repetition of the Names of Unity by the tongue of the secret being, without letters and without sound. As Allah (Exalted is He) has said in the Sacred Tradition [Hadith Qudsi]:

The human being is My secret, and I am his secret.

He has also said (Almighty and Glorious is He):

Knowledge of the inner being is one of My secrets. I have installed it in the heart of My servants, and no one is aware of it, apart from Me.

-and He has said (Exalted is He):

I am as My servant thinks of Me, and I am with him when he remembers Me. If he remembers Me in private, I remember him within Myself. If he remembers me in company, I remember him in better company.

The practice of reflection [tafakkur] is essential in this context. As the Prophet said (blessing and peace be upon him):

A moment of reflection is worth more than a year of worship.

A moment of reflection is worth more than a seventy years of worship.

A moment of reflection is worth more than a thousand years of worship.

These sayings convey the implicit meaning:

If someone reflects on the details of the branches [of knowledge], a moment of reflection is worth more than a year of worship.

If someone reflects for a moment on the true significance of the worship incumbent upon him, that is worth more than seventy years of worship.

If someone reflects for a moment on intimate knowledge of Allah (Exalted is He), that is worth more than a thousand years of worship.

Through intimate knowledge ['irfan], meaning the realization of Oneness, the 'arif [intimate knower] attains to his Ma'ruf [the One he knows intimately] and his Beloved, so he flies with spiritual wings to the realm of Nearness. The worshipful servant walks on foot to the Garden of Paradise, while the intimate knower flies on wings to the Nearness [of the Lord]. In the words of a poet:

The hearts of lovers have eyes. They see what other watchers fail to see. With featherless wings they fly to the Realm of the Lord of the Worlds.

This soaring flight takes place in the inner core of the intimate knower, who is the real human being, the dear friend of Allah (Almighty and Glorious is He), as sacred to Him as a bride. According to Abu Yazid al-Bistami: "Allah's people are the brides of Allah." Allah's saints [awliya'] have also been described as the brides of Allah. The point is that these "brides" are secluded by the veil of intimacy, visible to no one but Allah (Exalted is He). In the Sacred Tradition [Hadith Qudsi], He has said (Almighty and Glorious is He):

My saints are underneath My gown. No one is aware of them apart from Me.

All that people notice about the bride is the beauty of her outward appearance.

According to Yahya ibn Mu'adh ar-Razi: "The saint [wali] is the perfume of Allah upon the earth. The champions of the Truth detect its fragrance." Its scent reaches their hearts, so it makes them yearn for their Master. Their devotion to worship increases in proportion to the annihilation of their ordinary natures, because nearness increases as extinction increases. The saint becomes extinct to his worldly condition, and survives in witnessing the Truth. He retains no personal volition, and has no residence with anyone other than Allah. He has charismatic powers at his disposal, but he stays aloof from them, because he sees what others do not see, and regards divulging the secret of Lordship as an act of infidelity [kufr].

As we read in the book called al-Mirsad: "All those endowed with charismatic powers are veiled from sight. For such men, the charismatic marvel is a form of menstruation. The saint has a thousand stages to traverse, the first of them being the gate of charismatic marvels. If he passes beyond it safely, he can reach the other stages, but if not, he can make no further progress."

SECOND SECTION

The Reduction Of The Human Being To The Lowest Of The Low.

Allah created the holy spirit in the finest formation in the realm of Divinity [Lahut]. Then He wished to reduce it to the lowest of the low, for the purpose of increasing intimacy and nearness:

In a sure abode, in the presence of a King All-Powerful. fi maq'adi sidqin 'inda Malikin Muqtadir. (54:55)

That is the station of the saints and the Prophets.

He sent it down first to the realm of Omnipotence [Jabarut], and with it He sent the seed of the affirmation of Oneness [Tawhid]. He endowed it with the radiance of that realm, and clothed it with the appropriate attire. Then, when He sent it down to the realm of Dominion [Mulk], He created for it a material raiment, meaning this coarse body, so that the realm of Dominion would not be scorched by it.

In the context of the realm of Omnipotence [Jabarut], the spirit is called a royal spirit. In the context of the realm of Sovereignty [Malakut], it is called a travelling and freely moving spirit. In the context of the realm of Dominion [Mulk], it is called a physical spirit.

The purpose of its coming to the lowest realm is that it should gain extra nearness and degree of progress, by means of the heart [qalb] and the mold [qalab]. The seed of the affirmation of Oneness is planted in the ground of the heart, so that the tree of Oneness will grow there, with its root firmly established and it branches bearing the fruits of Oneness in the atmosphere of joy, for the good pleasure of Allah (Exalted is He). The seed of the Sacred Law is also planted in the ground of the heart, so that the tree of the Sacred Law will grow there, bearing the fruits of the degrees of progress.

Allah (Exalted is He) commanded all the spirits to enter the physical body, so He allotted each one of them a place therein. The place of the physical spirit is between the flesh and the blood. The place of the holy spirit is the innermost being. Each of them has a shop [hanut] in the town of existence, as well as goods, profits, and a commerce that is always lucrative, both secretly and openly.

They hope for a commerce that will never be unprofitable. yarjuna tijaratan lan tabur. (35:29)

It is therefore incumbent on every human being to know and understand his business in the sphere of his existence, because whatever he acquires here will be fastened to his neck. As Allah (Exalted is He) has said:

Does he not know when the contents a-fa-la ya'lamu idha bu'thira of the tombs are poured forth, ma fi'l-qubur: and that which is in the breasts is brought out? wa hussila ma fi's-sudur. (100: 9,10)

And We have fastened every man's bird of omen wa kulla insanin alzamna-hu ta'ira-hu to his own neck. fi 'unuqi-h. (17:13)

THIRD SECTION

The Shops Of The Spirit In The Body.

The shop [hanut] of the physical spirit consists of the breast, together with the external limbs and organs of the body. Its merchandise is the Sacred Law, and its business is performance of the duties Allah has commanded, by observing the external rules and without attributing partners to Him. As Allah (Exalted is He) has said:

And let him give no one any share at all in the worship due unto his Lord. wa la yushrik bi-'ibadati Rabbi-hi ahada. (18:110)

Allah is Single, and He loves that which is single. That is to say, He loves work that is sincerely devoted to Him, without hypocritical display and the pursuit of fame.

The profit [from this business] in this world consists of sainthood, mystic disclosure and direct vision in the realm of Dominion [Mulk], from the ground underfoot to heaven above. It may take the form of charismatic marvels, like walking on water, flying through the air, covering great distance with a single stride, hearing from afar, seeing what is hidden inside the body, and so on.

As for its profit in the Hereafter, it consists of the gardens, the houries, the palaces, the manservants, the drinks, and all the bounties in the first Garden, which is the Garden of Shelter [Jannat al-Ma'wa].

The shop of the freely moving spirit is the heart. Its merchandise is knowledge of the Spiritual Path, and its business is its preoccupation with the first four Names [of Allah]. These are among the twelve roots of the Names, which have no pronunciation and no alphabetic spelling. As Allah (Exalted is He) has said:

Say: "Cry to Allah, or cry to the All-Merciful. quli'd'u'llaha awi'd'u'r-Rahman: To whichever you cry, ayyam-ma tad'u His are the Most Beautiful Names." fa-la-hu'l-Asma'u'l-Husna. (17:110)

To Allah belong the Most Beautiful Names, wali'llahi'l-Asma'u'l-Husna so invoke Him by them. fa-'d'u-hu bi-ha. (7:180)

These are indications that the Names are central to the main preoccupation, which is knowledge of the inner being. Direct knowledge is the product of the Names of Oneness. The Prophet (peace be upon him) said:

Allah (Exalted is He) has ninety-nine Names. Anyone who counts them will enter the Garden of Paradise.

He also said (peace be upon him):

The lesson is one, and the repetition is a thousand.

What is meant by "counting" the Names is that one should come to be characterized by them, and moulded by their qualities.

These twelve Names are the roots of the Names of Allah (Exalted is He), based on the number of the Arabic letters in la ilaha illa'llah [There is no god but Allah]. The letters of this sentence are twelve [in the Arabic script]. For each letter, Allah has thus established one Name in the layers of the heart, three Names in each realm. Allah has thereby confirmed the hearts of the lovers. As Allah (Exalted is He) has said:

Allah confirms those who believe, yuthabbitu'lla-hu'lladhina amanu with the Word that stands firm, bi'l-qawli'th-thabiti in the life of this world and in the Hereafter. fi'l-hayati'd-dunya wa fi'l-akhira. (14:27)

Allah has sent down upon them the tranquillity of intimate friendship, and Allah has firmly established the tree of the affirmation of Oneness. The root of that tree is firmly planted in the seventh [level of the] earth, in the very ground beneath us, and its branches spread in the heaven above, extending beyond the Throne. Allah (Exalted is He) has said:

Do you not see how Allah coins a similitude: a-lam tara kaifa daraba'llahu mathalan A good saying, like a good tree, kalimatan tayyibatan ka-shajaratin tayyibatin its roots set firm, aslu-ha thabitun and its branches reaching into heaven? wa far'u-ha fi's-sama'. (14:24)

The profit of this shop is the life of the heart. The freely moving spirit enjoys direct vision in the realm of Sovereignty [Malakut], where it witnesses the Gardens, their radiant lights and their angels. Its speech is the speech of the inner being, and it considers the inner Names without sound or spelling. Its abode in the Hereafter is in the second Garden, which is the Garden of Bliss.

The shop of the royal spirit is the heart's core. Its merchandise is direct knowledge, and its business is constant attention to the four Names, expressed in the language of the heart. As the Prophet (peace be upon him) once said:

Knowledge ['ilm] is two-fold: knowledge conveyed by the tongue, that being Allah's testimony to His servants, and knowledge conveyed by the heart, that being the knowledge that is useful, because knowledge provides benefits in this sphere.

He also said (peace be upon him):

The Qur'an has an outer meaning and an inner meaning.

-and he said (peace be upon him):

Allah sent down the Qur'an in ten successive layers of inner meaning. Each inner meaning is more useful and more profitable than the one before, because it is a marrow [mukhkh].

These Names are comparable to the twelve springs that gushed forth when Moses (peace be upon him) struck the rock with his staff. Allah (Exalted is He) has said:

And when Moses asked for water for his people, wa idhi'stasqa Musa li-qawmi-hi We said: "Smite the rock with your staff." fa-qulna'drib bi-'asa-ka'l-hajar: And there gushed out from it twelve springs. fa'nfajarat min-hu'thnata 'ashrata 'aina: Each tribe knew their drinking-place. qad 'alima kullu unasin mashraba-hum. (2:60)

Exoteric knowledge is like spasmodic rain, while esoteric knowledge is more useful, since it is like an inexhaustible fountain. Allah (Exalted is He) has said:

And a sign to them is the dead earth. wa ayatun la humu'l-ardu'l-maita: We revive it, and We bring forth from it grain ahyaina-ha wa akhrajna min-ha habban so that they eat thereof. fa-min-hu ya'kulun. (36:33)

Allah (Exalted is He) brought forth the horizons from the earth, as a grain that is the strength of the animal natures. He also brought forth from the earth the personal identities [of human beings], as a grain that is the strength of the spiritual spirits [arwah ruhaniyya]. The Prophet (peace be upon him) said:

If someone is sincerely devoted to Allah (Exalted is He) for forty mornings, the fountains of wisdom will flow from his heart to his tongue.

As for the profit of this shop, it is the vision of the reflection of Allah's Beauty (Exalted is He). Allah (Exalted is He) has said:

One of mighty power has taught him, 'allama-hu Shadidu'l-quwwa: One of great vigour; and he grew clear to view, Dhu mirra: fa-'stawa when he was on the highest horizon. wa huwa bi'l-ufuqi'l-a'la Then he drew near and came down, thumma dana fa-tadalla till he was two bows' length or nearer, fa-kana qaba qawsaini aw adna and He revealed to His servant that which He revealed. fa-awha ila 'abdi-hi ma awha. The heart in no way falsified what he saw. ma kadhaba'l-fu'adu mara'a. (53:5-11)

The Prophet (peace be upon him) said:

The faithful is the mirror of the Faithful [al-mu'minu mir'atu'l-Mu'min].

The first "faithful" is the heart of the faithful servant, while the second is Allah (Exalted is He). Allah has described Himself (Exalted is He) as:

The Faithful, the Guardian....[u]'l-Mu'minu'l-Muhaiminu.... (59:23)

The final abode of this group is in the third Garden, which is Paradise [Firdaws].

The shop of the holy spirit is inside the secret being. As Allah (Exalted is He) has said:

The human being is My secret and I am his secret.

Its merchandise is the knowledge of Reality [Haqiqa], that being the knowledge of Oneness. Its business is the constant repetition of the Names of Oneness, they being the last four, with a speechless tongue. Allah (Exalted is He) has said:

And if you speak aloud, wa in tajhar bi'l-qawli He surely knows the secret fa-inna-hu ya'lamu's-sirra and that which is yet more deeply hidden. wa akhfa. (20:7)

-so no one is aware of it, other than Allah (Exalted is He).

As for the profit of this shop, it is the emergence of the child of inner meanings, its direct witnessing and vision, and its lawful contemplation of Allah's countenance (Exalted is He) with the eye of the secret being:

That day will faces be resplendent, wujuhun yawma'idhin nadira: looking toward their Lord. ila Rabbi-ha nazira. (75:22,23)

-without "how?", without qualification and without comparison. As Allah (Exalted is He) has said:

There is nothing like unto Him, laisa ka-mithli-hi shai': and He is the All-Hearing, the All-Seeing. wa Huwa's-Sami'u'l-Basir. (42:11)

When the human being reaches his goal, minds become constricted, hearts become perplexed and tongues become exhausted. He cannot give any account of that experience, because Allah (Exalted is He) is exempt from all likenesses. When such accounts do reach the scholars, they must therefore base their understanding on the various levels of knowledge, seek to grasp their real meanings, and turn their attention toward the highest heights. They must strive to attain to knowledge of the Divine Presence and understanding of the Singular Essence, without rejecting and denying the explanation we have given.

FOURTH SECTION

The Number Of The Sciences ['Ulum].

Explanation of the Sacred Law [Shari'a], the Spiritual Path [Tariqa], Direct Knowledge [Ma'rifa] and Reality [Haqiqa].

Exoteric science [al-'ilm az-zahir] consists of twelve branches, and esoteric science [al-'ilm al-batin] likewise has twelve branches. These branches are divided among the common folk and the special elite, in proportion to their capability.

The sciences ['ulum] are grouped in four sections:

1. The outer aspect of the Sacred Law [Shari'a], meaning the commandments, prohibitions, and other rules and regulations.

2. The inner aspect of the Sacred Law, which I have called the Science of the Inner and the Spiritual Path [Tariqa].

3. Esotericism, which I have called the Science of Direct Knowledge [Ma'rifa].

4. The innermost of inner factors, which I have called the Science of Reality [Haqiqa].

It is essential to acquire knowledge of all these sciences, for, as the Prophet (peace be upon him) said:

The Sacred Law is a tree, the Spiritual Path is its branches, Direct Knowledge is its leaves, and Reality is its fruit.

The Qur'an contains them all, explicitly and by implication, by commentary or by interpretation. According to the author of al-Majma': "Commentary [tafsir] is for the common folk, while interpretation [ta'wil] is for the elite, because they are the scholars who are rooted [rasikhun] in knowledge. The meaning of 'rootedness [rusukh]' is 'firmness, establishment and commitment' to knowledge, just as the root of the palm tree is firmly established in the earth, while its branches reach up into the sky. This rootedness is the result of the profession [that there is no god except Allah] that is planted in the core of the heart after purification. [In the following Qur'anic verse] Allah (Exalted is He) has referred to 'those who are rooted in knowledge' immediately after His saying (Almighty and Glorious is He) 'except Allah [illa'llah]':

"He it is who has sent down to you the Book Huwa'lladhi anzala 'alai-ka'l-Kitaba wherein are clear signs-they are the min-hu ayatun muhkamatun hunna substance of the Book-and others allegorical. Ummu'l-Kitabi wa ukharu mutashabihat: But those in whose hearts is doubt fa-amma'lladhina fi qulubi-him zaighun pursue that which is allegorical, fa-yattabi'una ma tashabaha seeking dissension by seeking its interpretation. min-hu 'btigha'a'l-fitnati wa'btigha'a ta'wili-h: None knows its interpretation except Allah. wa ma ya'lamu ta'wila-hu illa'llah: And those who are rooted in knowledge say: wa'r-rasikhuna fi'l-'ilmi yaquluna We believe therein; the whole is from our Lord. 'amanna bi-hi kullun min'indi Rabbi-na: But only men of understanding really heed. wa ma yadhdhakkaru illa ulu'l-albab. (3:7)"

According to the author of at-Tafsir al-Kabir [The Great Commentary]: "If this door were opened, the doors of the inner mysteries would open too."

The servant is also commanded to observe the commandment and the prohibition, and to oppose the lower self [nafs] in each of the four spheres. In the sphere of the Sacred Law, the lower self insinuates contradictions. In the sphere of the Spiritual Path, it insinuates deceptive conformities, like the claim to Prophethood and sainthood. In the sphere of Direct Knowledge, it insinuates concealed polytheism [shirk khafi] in the guise of luminous revelations, like the claim to Lordship. As Allah (Exalted is He) has said:

Have you seen him who chooses a-ra'aita mani'ttakhadha for his god his own lust? ilaha-hu hawa-h. (25:43)

As for the sphere of Reality, the devil has no access to it, nor does the lower self, nor do the angels, because anyone other than Allah is (Exalted is He) is burned to ashes therein. As Gabriel (peace be upon him) said: "If I had drawn nearer by a fingertip, I would surely have burned to ashes." [In this sphere] the servant is therefore uninfluenced by two opponents [the devil and his own lower self], and he is sincerely devoted [to Allah]. As Allah (Exalted is He) has said:

[Satan] said: "Then, by Your might, qala fa-bi'Izzati-ka, I shall surely beguile them every one, la-ughwiyanna-hum ajma'in. except Your sincerely devoted servants among them." illa 'ibada-ka min-humu'l-mukhlasin. (38:82,83)

So long as he has not attained to Reality, the servant cannot be sincerely devout, because the disloyal human attributes will only be annihilated by the manifestation of the Divine Essence, and ignorance will only be removed by direct knowledge of the Divine Essence (Glory be to Him and Exalted is He). Allah (Exalted is He) will teach him an esoteric knowledge from His Presence, without intermediary, so he will come to know Him through His instruction, and worship Him through His teaching, as in the case of al-Khidr (peace be upon him).

Once he has reached this stage, the servant will witness the holy spirits. He will come to know his Prophet Muhammad (Allah bless him and give him peace), who will tell him about everything from the beginning to the end, and all the other Prophets will give him glad tidings of the eternal communion. As Allah (Exalted is He) has said:

And whoever obeys Allah and the Messenger, wa man yuti'i'llaha they are in the company of those wa'r-rasula fa-ula'ika ma'a'lladhina to whom Allah has granted gracious favouran'ama'llahu 'alai-him the Prophets, the champions of truth, the martyrs mina'n-nabiyyina wa's-siddiqina wa'sh-shuhada'i and the righteous-and the best of company are they!" wa's-salihin: wa hasuna ula'ika rafiqa. (4:69)

If someone has not acquired this knowledge, he is not a scholar in reality, even if he has read a million books. In as much as he does not reach the spiritual level, though he performs physical work in accordance with the outer aspects of the sciences, his recompense will be the Garden of Paradise, and that alone. Only the reflection of the [Divine] attributes will be manifest there. The scholar does not gain access, by exoteric knowledge alone, to the Holy Sanctuary and nearness [to the Lord], because that is the realm of flight, and birds do not fly without wings.

If the servant acts in accordance with both exoteric and esoteric knowledge, he will reach that realm. As Allah (Exalted is He) has said in the Sacred Tradition [Hadith Qudsi]:

O My servant, if you wish to enter My sanctuary, you must pay no attention to the dominion [of this world], the realm of Sovereignty [Malakut] and the realm of Omnipotence [Jabarut], because the dominion [of this world] is the devil of the scholar, the realm of Sovereignty is the devil of the direct knower, and the realm of Omnipotence is the devil of the overseer.

If someone takes notice of any one of these temptations, he is an outcast in the sight of Allah (Exalted is He), meaning an outcast from nearness, not an outcast from the abode. Such are those who seek nearness, but fail to reach it, because they are distracted by desire, and because they only have one wing.

As for the people of nearness, they receive that which no eye has ever seen, of which no ear has ever heard, and which has never occurred to a human heart. That is the Garden of Nearness, in which there are no houries and no palaces.

The human being needs to recognize his true value, and he must not claim for himself what is not his right and proper due. It was 'Ali (may Allah ennoble his countenance) who said: "May Allah have mercy on a man who knows his own worth, who does not go beyond his limit, who guards his tongue, and who does not waste his life."

The scholar must therefore comprehend the meaning of the reality of the human being, called the child of inner meanings. He must train that child to practice constant affirmation of the Names of Oneness, and to leave the realm of physicality for the realm of spirituality, which is the realm of mystery, where there are no abodes except Allah. That realm is like a desert of light, to which there is no end. The child of inner meanings flies over it, and beholds its strange and marvellous wonders, but they are impossible to describe. It is the place of those affirmers of Oneness who lost their own identity in the eye of Singularity. The sight of Allah's Beauty left them with no existence in the meantime, just as staring at the sun makes everything else invisible. Without a doubt, the human being cannot see himself at the same time as Allah's Beauty, because of the overwhelming astonishment and fascination.

As Jesus (peace be upon him) said: "The human being does not enter the Kingdom of the Heavens, unless he is born twice, as the birds are born twice." This refers to the birth of the child of spiritual meanings from the reality of human capability. That is the secret of the human being. It is conceived and born from the union of the science of the Sacred Law and the science of Reality, just as the ordinary child results from the union of the two sperms from the man and the woman. As Allah (Exalted is He) has said:

We created the human being from a sperm-drop, inna khalaqna'l-insana min nutfatin a mingling, in order to try him; amshajin nabtali-h: and We made him hearing, seeing. fa-ja'alna-hu sami'an basira. (76:2)

After the manifestation of this inner meaning, it becomes a simple matter to pass from the surface of the oceans of creation to the depths of the commandment. In comparison with the realm of the spirit, every other realm is like a drop of water. After that [manifestation], the spiritual and esoteric sciences are communicated without a letter [of the alphabet] and without a sound.

FIFTH SECTION

Repentance [Tawba] And Verbal Instruction [Talqin].

You should know that the above-mentioned stages [of spiritual progress] can only be attained through genuine repentance [tawba nasuh], and with verbal instruction [talqin] from qualified experts. As Allah (Exalted is He) has said:

And He imposed on them wa alzama-hum the profession of true devotion. kalimata't-taqwa. (48:26)

That is the profession: "There is no god but Allah [la ilaha illa'llah]," with the stipulation that it must come from a heart that is truly devout, pure of everything apart from Allah, not like any statement heard from the mouths of the common folk. The wording may be the same in each case, but there is a difference in the meaning.

The heart is enlivened only when it receives the seed of the affirmation of Oneness from a living heart. It must be a perfect seed, for nothing grows from a seed that is immature. That is why Allah sent down the profession of Oneness [kalimat at-Tawhid] in two places in the Qur'an, once in connection with the outer expression:

When it was said to them: inna-hum kanu idha qila la-hum "There is no god but Allah," la ilaha illa'llahu they were scornful, and they said: yastakbirun: wa yaquluna "Shall we forsake our gods?" a-inna la-tariku alihati-na. (37:35,36)

-and once in connection with real knowledge:

So know that there is no god but Allah, fa-'lam anna-hu la ilaha illa'llahu and ask forgiveness for your sin, wa'staghfir li-dhanbi-ka and for the believing men and believing women. wali'l-mu'minina wa'l-mu'minat: Allah knows your going to and from, wa'llahu ya'lamu mutaqabbala-kum and your lodging. wa mathwa-kum. (47:19)

This instruction [talqin], concerning the reason for the revelation of this noble Qur'anic verse [aya], is for the benefit of the special few.

According to the author of Bustan ash-Shari'a [The Orchard of the Sacred Law]: "'Ali (may Allah be well pleased with him) was the first to ask the Prophet (Allah bless him and give him peace) to show him the nearest, the finest and the easiest of the spiritual paths. The Prophet (Allah bless him and give him peace) waited for inspiration [wahy], so Gabriel (peace be upon him) came down and instructed him to repeat this profession [of Oneness] three times. The Prophet (Allah bless him and give him peace) then said what Gabriel (peace be upon him) had told him to say. The Prophet (Allah bless him and give him peace) then instructed 'Ali (may Allah be well pleased with him) to do likewise. Then he came to his Companions and gave the same instruction to them all."

[In the wake of a battle with the unbelievers], the Prophet (Allah bless him and give him peace) said [to his Companions]:

We have come home from the lesser sacred struggle [al-jihad al-asghar]. We are returning to the greater sacred struggle [al-jihad al-akbar].

-meaning the sacred struggle with the lower self [jihad an-nafs]. As the Prophet (Allah bless him and give him peace) said to one of his Companions:

The greatest of all your enemies is that lower self of yours, in there between your flanks.

The love of Allah will not be experienced until His enemies, the instigating self [an-nafs al-ammara], the censorious self [lawwama] and the inspiring self [mulhima], have been conquered in your being. You must purify your being of the blameworthy characteristics of domestic animals, like the love of excessive eating, drinking, sleep and idle play, and of those of savage beasts, like anger, abuse, assault and coercion. You must also purify your being of satanic characteristics, like arrogant pride, vain conceit, envy and malice, and of other such vices of the body and the heart. Once you are cleansed of these impurities, you will be cleansed of the root of sins, and you will be included among those who purify themselves and are truly repentant.

Allah loves those who are truly repentant, inna'llaha yuhibbu't-tawwabina and He loves those who purify themselves. wa yuhibbu'l-mutatahhirin. (2:222)

If someone repents, but only of the outer aspect of sins, the obvious conclusion is that he is not covered by this Qur'anic verse [aya], since he is ta'ib [simply repentant], but not tawwab [utterly repentant]. The form tawwab is intensive, so it refers to the repentance of the special few. If someone repents, but only of the outer aspect of sins, he is like someone who cuts the grass above the ground, and does not take the trouble to dig it out by the roots, so it is sure to grow again, even more thickly than before.

As for someone who is truly repentant of all sins and blameworthy traits of character, his likeness is that of someone who digs the grass out by its roots, so it will certainly not grow again, except in very rare cases. After true repentance, therefore, the necessary instruction [talqin] is to uproot everything apart from Allah (Exalted is He) from the heart. If the bitter trees are not uprooted, the sweet trees will not take their place.

You must therefore pay careful attention, O possessors of perceptive faculties, for then you may prosper and succeed. Allah (Exalted is He) has said:

And He is the One who accepts repentance wa Huwa'lladhi yaqbalu't-tawbata from His servants, and pardons evil deeds, 'an 'ibadi-hi wa ya'fu 'ani's-sayyi'ati and He knows what you are doing. wa ya'lamu ma taf'alun. (42:25)

He has also said (Glory be to Him):

Except those who repent, and believe, illa man taba wa amana and do righteous work-wa'amila 'amalan salihan in their case, Allah will change fa-ula'ika yubaddilu'llahu their evil deeds into good deeds, sayyi'ati-him hasanat: for Allah is ever All-Forgiving, All-Compassionate. wa kana'llahu Ghafuran Rahima. (25:70)

Repentance is of two kinds: the repentance of the common folk [tawbat al-'amm] and the repentance of the special few [tawbat al-khawass]:

1. The repentance of the common folk is returning from sinful disobedience to worshipful obedience, from what is blameworthy to that which is praiseworthy, from the Inferno to the Garden, from the comfort of the body to the hardship of [conflict with] the lower self, by means of remembrance [dhikr], dedicated striving and vigorous endeavour.

2. The repentance of the special few is returning, after the achievement of this repentance, from the virtues of the pious to the sources of direct knowledge, from the stages of progress to nearness, and from physical pleasures to spiritual pleasures. That means forsaking everything apart from Allah (Exalted is He), enjoying intimacy with Him, and viewing Him with the eye of certitude.

To enjoy the benefits of material existence is to be guilty of sin. In the words of the saying addressed to the Prophet (Allah bless him and give him peace):

Your material existence is such a sin that no other sin can be compared with it.

According to the great elders (may Allah the Exalted bestow His mercy upon them): "The good deeds of the pious are the bad deeds of those drawn near [to the Lord]." That is why the Prophet (Allah bless him and give him peace) used to seek Allah's forgiveness one hundred times each day, as Allah (Exalted is He) told him:

And ask forgiveness for your sin. wa'staghfir li-dhanbi-ka. (47:19)

That is to say: "for the sin of your material existence." This is the repentance called inaba, which means returning to Allah (Exalted is He) from everything apart from Him, entering into the safety of nearness in the Hereafter, and beholding the Countenance of Allah (Exalted is He). As the Prophet (Allah bless him and give him peace) once said:

Allah (Exalted is He) has servants whose bodies are in this world, while their hearts are beneath the Heavenly Throne.

The vision of Allah (Exalted is He) is impossible in this world, where it is possible only to view the attributes of Allah (Exalted is He) in the mirror of the heart. It was 'Umar (may Allah be well pleased with him) who said: "My heart saw my Lord by the light of my Lord." The heart is a mirror in which the Beauty of Allah (Exalted is He) is reflected.

This witnessing [of the Divine attributes] is attainable only through the instruction [talqin] of an accomplished Shaikh, one who has been accepted among the predecessors, then sent back here to perfect the deficient, at the command of Allah (Exalted is He), in accordance with the example of the Prophet (Allah bless him and give him peace). The saints (may Allah the Exalted be well pleased with them) are sent to the special few, not to the common folk. This is the difference between the Prophet and the saint [wali]: The Prophet is sent to the common folk and the special few alike, and he is free to set his own independent example, whereas the spiritual guide [murshid] is sent only to the special few, and he is not free to set his own independent example, because he qualified only to follow his Prophet (peace be upon him). If he did claim independence, he would be guilty of unbelief [kufr].

When the Prophet (Allah bless him and give him peace) made the comparison:

The scholars of my Community are like the Prophets of the Children of Israel.

-he did so because they [those Prophets] were the loyal followers of the Sacred Law of the Messenger, he being Moses (blessing and peace be upon him). Their task was to renew that Law and confirm its rules, without introducing another Sacred Law.

The same is true of the scholars of this Islamic Community, inasmuch as the saints are sent to the special few, in order to renew the commandment and the prohibition, to establish right practice with the utmost support, and to purify the basis of the Sacred Law, which is the site of direct knowledge in the heart. They transmit knowledge of the Prophet (Allah bless him and give him peace), just as the Companions of the Bench [Ashab as-Suffa] used to tell of the mysteries of the Heavenly Ascension [Mi'raj], even before the Prophet (Allah bless him and give him peace) reported the news. The saint is the bearer of the sainthood [wilaya] of the Prophet (Allah bless him and give him peace), which is an element of his Prophethood, and his inner being is entrusted to his guardianship.

This does not apply to all those [scholars of the Community] who follow the outer aspect of knowledge, because they may be heirs of the Prophet, but only as relatives on the maternal side. The complete heir is one who is in the position of the son, because that is the closest of paternal relationships. The son is the father's secret being, both outwardly and inwardly. That is why the Prophet (blessing and peace be upon him) once said:

Some knowledge is like the form of the hidden treasure. It is known only by those who truly know Allah (Exalted is He). When they speak of it, the people of honour cannot deny it.

This is the secret that was lodged in the heart of the Prophet (Allah bless him and give him peace) on the night of the Heavenly Ascension, in the innermost of the thirty thousand inner compartments. He did not reveal it to any of the common folk, but only to his closest Companions and the Companions of the Bench. The blessing of that secret is the implementation of the Sacred Law until the Day of Resurrection.

Esoteric knowledge guides one to that secret, for all the academic sciences and skills are the shell of that secret. As for the exoteric scholars, they are inheritors, so some of them are in the position of the owner of material properties, and some are in the position of relatives on the maternal side. They rely on the shells of knowledge, in order to summon people to Allah (Exalted is He) with good advice. The Sunni Shaikhs are linked by their spiritual chain [silsila] to 'Ali (may Allah be well pleased with him), at the station of knowledge at the gate of knowledge, inviting people to Allah (Blessed and Exalted is He) and giving wise advice. As Allah (Exalted is He) has said:

Summon to the way of your Lord with wisdom ud'u ila sabili Rabbi-ka bi'l-hikmati and good admonition, wa'l-maw'izati'l-hasanati and dispute with them in the better way. wa jadil-hum bi'llati hiya ahsan. (16:125)

What they [the Shaikhs] say is basically the same, though there may be differences in detail.

Three meaningful elements are combined in the Qur'anic verse [aya], and they are likewise combined in the essential nature of the Prophet (Allah bless him and give him peace). No one can carry all that after him, so it is divided into three parts:

1. Knowledge of the spiritual state [hal]. This is the kernel, which is granted to real men, and which is the aspiration of real men. As the Prophet (Allah bless him and give him peace) once said:

The aspiration of real men is the uprooting of the mountains.

What is meant by the mountains is the hardness of the heart, which is eradicated by their supplication and their humble appeal. As Allah (Blessed and Exalted is He) has said:

He gives wisdom to whomever He will, yu'ti'l-hikmata man yasha': and he to whom wisdom is given, wa man yu'ta'l-hikmata he has truly received abundant good. fa-qad utiya khairan kathira. (2:269)

2. The second part is the shell of that kernel, which is given to the exoteric scholars. It consists of good advice, commanding what is right and proper, and forbidding what is wrong and improper. As the Prophet (blessing and peace be upon him) once said:

The scholar preaches with knowledge and good manners, while the ignoramus preaches with aggressiveness and anger.

3. The third part is the shell of the shell, which is given to the worldly rulers. It consists of external justice and the government indicated by His saying (Blessed and Exalted is He):

And dispute with them in the better way. wa jadil-hum bi'llati hiya ahsan. (16:125)

The worldly rulers possess the outer means of control, and the means to preserve the good order of the religion, like the red shell [the husk that protects the shell]. The esoteric scholars are like the kernel within the shell.

The Prophet (blessing and peace be upon him) once said:

You must frequent the company of the scholars, and listen to the speech of the wise. Allah (Exalted is He) revives the heart with the light of wisdom, just as He revives the dead earth with the water of rain.

He also said (blessing and peace be upon him):

The word of wisdom is wandering astray. The wise man snatches it wherever he finds it.

The words in the mouths of the common folk have come down from the Well-kept Tablet [al-Lawh al-Mahfuz], which is on the level of the realm of Omnipotence [Jabarut]. The words in the mouths of real men, those men who have reached their goal, have come down from the Greatest Tablet on the tongue of Holiness, without intermediary in the realm of Nearness.

Everything must return to its original source. That is why it is a compulsory duty to seek the expert instructors, for the sake of the life of the heart. As the Prophet (blessing and peace be upon him) once said:

The quest for knowledge is a strict obligation for every Muslim man and Muslim woman.

That knowledge is the knowledge of direct experience and nearness. As for the rest, there is no need for the exoteric sciences, except when they contribute to the performance of religious duties, like the science of jurisprudence [fiqh] in relation to acts of worship. As al-Ghazali (may Allah be well pleased with him) said in poetry:

The life of the heart is knowledge, so preserve it, The death of the heart is ignorance, so avoid it.

Your best provision is true devotion, so provide it. This advice of mine is enough for you, so heed it.

Allah (Blessed and Exalted is He) is well pleased with those of His servants who make the transition to nearness, and attach no importance to degrees of rank. As Allah (Blessed and Exalted is He) has said:

Say: "I do not ask of you a fee for it, qul la as'alu-kum 'alai-hi ajran except love in close kinship." illa'l-mawaddata fi'l-qurba. (42:23)

In this context, according to one interpretation, what is meant by qurba [close kinship] is qurba [nearness (to the Lord)].